WHO BECAME FAMOUS DURING THE RENAISSANCE?

History Books for Kids
Children's Renaissance Books

BABY PROFESSOR
EDUCATION KIDS

Speedy Publishing LLC

40 E. Main St. #1156

Newark, DE 19711

www.speedypublishing.com

Copyright 2017

In this book, we're going to talk about who became famous during the Renaissance. So, let's get right to it!

The Renaissance was a wonderful golden age that spread from Italy throughout Europe. Culture in the form of literature, poetry, architecture, paintings, and sculpture thrived and new ideas blossomed. Science was emerging as were new forms of religion. The Humanist philosophy had a profound impact as well. Many people became famous during the Renaissance and their legacies live on today.

DANTE ALLIGHIERI

DANTE ALIGHERI
(1265 TO 1321)

Dante was a poet and philosopher who lived in Italy. He is best known for his epic poem called The Divine Comedy. Written in Italian in the first person, The Divine Comedy is a journey through the afterlife.

Dante travels through hell, then purgatory, and finally heaven. Virgil, the Roman poet, guides Dante through hell and purgatory, but in heaven he's reunited with his eternal love Beatrice as she guides him.

Drawings for Dante´s Divine Comedy

Johannes Gutenberg

JOHANNES GUTENBERG
(1395 TO 1468)

Gutenberg was a printer who invented a system of movable type and a mechanical printing press. Because of Gutenberg, people from all walks of life began to have access to books and knowledge that was previously reserved for members of the Church and the wealthy.

Unfortunately, Gutenberg was sued by his investor and lost a good deal of his business. He typeset and printed his masterpiece, the "forty-two-line" Gutenberg Bible before his business was overtaken by his investor Johann Fust and Fust's son-in-law. These new mechanically printed Bibles represented the first time anyone outside the Church could afford to buy a bible. Printing presses flourished in the decades after Gutenberg's death and books eventually became accessible to everyone.

Gutenberg Statue

Joan of Arc

JOAN OF ARC
(1412 TO 1431)

Joan of Arc was a peasant girl who had visions. Acting under what she felt was divine guidance from St. Michael and St. Catherine, she was told to obtain an audience with Charles who was the heir to the throne in France. She wanted to get his permission to drive the English out of France during the Hundred Years War.

Charles would then take the throne as king. Legend has it that when she met with Charles she told him details of a prayer he had said to God to help him save France. Joan was given the power to lead the French army to victory against the English. At 19 years of age, she was burned to death as a heretic by the English. She was made a saint by the Roman Catholic Church 500 years after her death.

Death of Joan of Arc

Mehmed II

MEHMED II
(1432 TO 1481)

Mehmed II, also known as Mehmed the Conqueror, brought an end to the Eastern Roman Empire when he invaded and conquered the city of Constantinople at the young age of 21. He also captured Anatolia as well as the Balkans, further strengthening the Ottoman Empire. He was Sultan of the Ottoman Empire from 1444 to 1446 and then for another 30 years from 1451 to 1481.

CHRISTOPHER COLUMBUS
(1451 TO 1506)

Italian explorer Christopher Columbus was looking for a new route to Asia or the East Indies by traveling westward when he discovered the Americas in 1492.

Christopher Columbus at the gates of the monastery

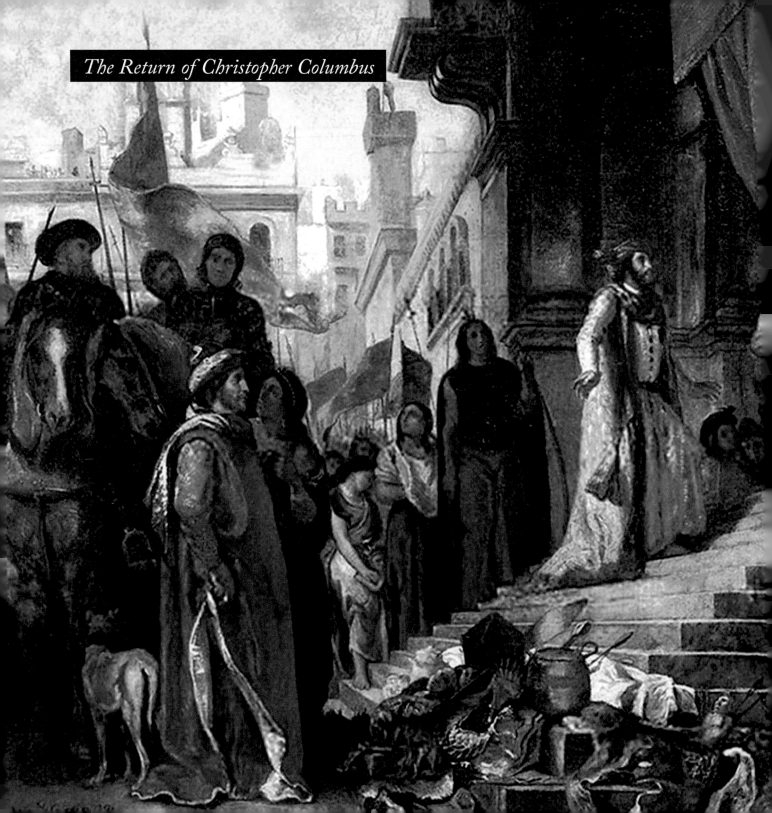

King Ferdinand and Queen Isabella sponsored his journey for the country of Spain. He was not the first European explorer to reach the Americas because the Vikings had been to the Americas in the 11th century, but his trips across the Atlantic opened up the Americas to European exploration.

LEONARDO DA VINCI
(1452 TO 1519)

Atrue Renaissance man, Leonardo was a master of many different forms of art. Though he didn't complete many paintings in his lifetime, the ones he completed are known as masterpieces today and were based on his many studies of human anatomy.

Profile Portrait of Leonardo Da Vinci

Mona Lisa

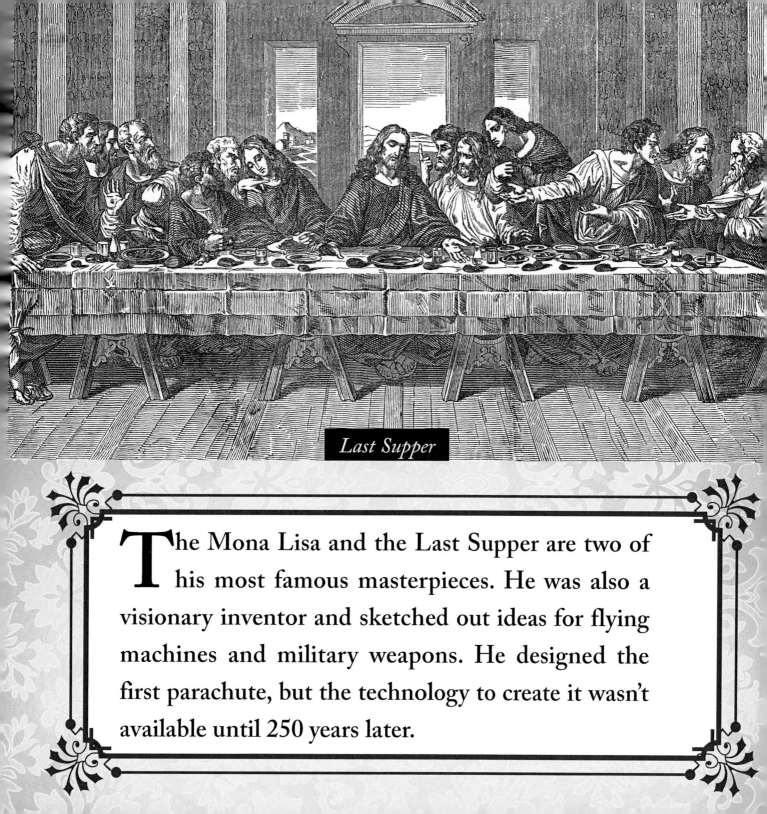

Last Supper

The Mona Lisa and the Last Supper are two of this most famous masterpieces. He was also a visionary inventor and sketched out ideas for flying machines and military weapons. He designed the first parachute, but the technology to create it wasn't available until 250 years later.

VASCO DA GAMA
(1460 TO 1524)

Indian spices were very popular in Europe. However, to get to India the journey had to be made over land. Portugal's king felt that there might be a way to find a route around the tip of Africa.

Vasco da Gama

The Departure of Vasco da Gama to India in 1497

He gave the explorer Vasco da Gama ships and men and asked him to find that route. Vasco was able to complete this dangerous expedition and came home a hero.

DESIDERIUS ERASMUS
(1468 TO 1536)

A Dutch scholar and priest, Desiderius Erasmus helped spread the philosophy of humanism throughout the northern part of Europe. He prepared important editions of the New Testament in Latin and Greek.

Portrait of Desiderius Erasmus

He was critical of some of the practices of the Catholic Church and this made his writings controversial. He wanted the Church to reform from within and didn't align himself with the teachings of Martin Luther. He was the author of a book that became well known during his lifetime called "Praise of Folly," which was a mixture of fantasy and satire.

MICHELANGELO
(1475 TO 1564)

One of the Renaissance period's most famous artists, Michelangelo became wealthy from his work, but often acted as if he were poor and slept in his clothes and boots. He was a masterful sculptor as well as a painter and poet.

Michelangelo

Michelangelo's Pieta

His masterpieces include the Pietà, which is a marble sculpture of the Virgin Mary holding the crucified Christ, the amazing frescoes of the Sistine Chapel, and the larger-than-life statue of David from the Old Testament.

MARTIN LUTHER
(1483 TO 1546)

Martin Luther was a German priest and scholar. He felt that the Catholic Church had abused its power. He was opposed to the Church asking for payments in return for giving people indulgences so they could get into heaven.

Martin Luther

Martin Luther and His Children

He wanted the teachings of the Bible to be available to all citizens so that they could fully understand Christ's teachings themselves. Luther's ideas eventually caused a time period called the Reformation. The results were Protestantism, a new form of Christian worship.

KING HENRY VIII
(1491 TO 1547)

At the beginning of his life, Henry VIII would have been considered a true Renaissance man. He was very athletic, handsome, and was an excellent horseman. He was also intelligent and spoke many languages. He was a musician and even composed some of his own music. A patron of the arts, Henry surrounded himself with artists and scholars from Europe.

King Henry VIII

When he was unable to have a male heir, he became unhappy with his marriage and wanted a divorce. The Catholic Church didn't allow divorce so he split with the Church. Over his lifetime, Henry had six wives. Three of the marriages were annulled, which means the Church agreed they were never marriages at all. He also beheaded two of his wives. When he was older, he became obese from overeating and couldn't walk because of ulcers in his legs.

PARACELSUS
(1493 TO 1541)

Abotanist as well as a doctor, Paracelsus was a pioneer in the advancement of medicine. After studying the results of many doctors' treatments, he found that they were actually making their patients feel worse instead of healing them. He did research to determine that diet and environment, as well as the proper treatment with drugs were all contributing factors to a patient's wellness.

Paracelsus

Catherine de Medici

CATHERINE DE MEDICI
(1519 TO 1589)

The Medici Family were powerful bankers and rulers of Florence during the Renaissance. When Catherine de Medici was just a girl she was kidnapped by enemies of her family. She told her kidnappers that she had planned to become a nun.

As a result of this quick answer, she was able to stay alive. After she was freed, she wed the King of France's son, Henry II. Henry II became France's king and Catherine had a great deal of power as France's queen. When Henry passed away from a terrible jousting accident, one of her sons took the throne. Eventually, another son became king of Poland and her daughter ruled Navarre.

King Henry II of France

Queen Elizabeth I

ELIZABETH I OF ENGLAND (1533 TO 1603)

Elizabeth I was the daughter of Henry VIII and his second wife Anne Boleyn. Elizabeth was only two years of age, when Henry had his Anne beheaded. She was declared illegitimate but eventually was able to gain power over the throne when she was twenty-five years of age. She was a strong queen and kept England safe and prosperous in Europe for over 44 years during her rule.

GALILEO
(1564 TO 1642)

Galileo was an Italian physicist and astronomer. He played a huge role in the scientific breakthroughs during the Renaissance. He was the first person to use a telescope to gaze at the heavens and he confirmed that the planet Venus had phases. He also discovered the four main moons of the planet Jupiter. Because of his studies in astronomy, he came to the conclusion that Copernicus had been correct in saying that the sun was at the center of the solar system.

Galileo Galilei

GALILEO

Portrait of William Shakespeare

WILLIAM SHAKESPEARE
(1564 TO 1616)

Amaster of the English language, Shakespeare wrote more than 37 plays and 885,000 words during his lifetime. His works are quoted almost as frequently as the Bible. Some of his most famous plays were Hamlet, Macbeth, and King Lear. Shakespeare became wealthy during his lifetime for his work and his plays are still performed today.

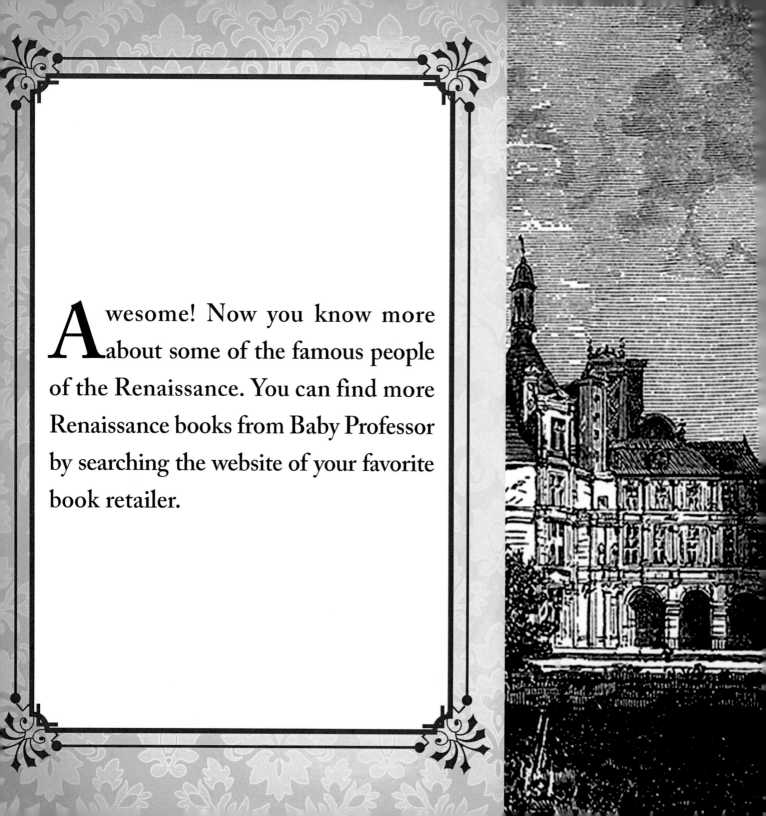

Awesome! Now you know more about some of the famous people of the Renaissance. You can find more Renaissance books from Baby Professor by searching the website of your favorite book retailer.

Visit

BABY PROFESSOR
EDUCATION KIDS

www.BabyProfessorBooks.com

to download Free Baby Professor eBooks
and view our catalog of new and exciting
Children's Books